Praise for the first edition

An attractive, sensitively written book that can help young children better understand their playmates and neighbors who may be of different faiths. Such an approach today helps ensure peace and cooperation tomorrow in our ever more diverse society.

—Joan Brown Campbell
General Secretary, National Council of
Churches in Christ in the USA

The concise, descriptive text and beautiful illustrations provide an informative and entertaining resource to help children—and adults—understand the diversity as well as the similarity of the world's religions.

—Jimmy Carter
39th President of the United States of America

At long last, a book that simply and accurately introduces children to many of the world's religious traditions. Teachers now have a lively and beautiful new resource for making sure that learning about religions is an important part of elementary education.

—Charles C. Haynes
Senior Scholar, Freedom Forum
First Amendment Center

A World of Faith introduces to young people the many different faiths that attract people of this universe towards God. I pray that it will lead to greater understanding on the part of our young people across the world.

—Theodore M. Hesburgh
President Emeritus, University of Notre Dame

A beautiful and elegant book that should be enjoyed by children and parents alike.

—Paul Kurtz
Publisher, *Free Inquiry* magazine

A World of Faith is an important book for all young people—a creative introduction to the great diversity of faith in our nation, which will help children view their world more openly. As president of NCCJ, an organization dedicated for over seventy years to fighting prejudice and promoting mutual respect among all, I am convinced that young readers of this book will look back years later and realize it was one of those critical first steps leading them to the path of greater interfaith understanding

—Sanford Cloud, Jr.
President and CEO,
National Conference for Community and Justice

A World of Faith

By Common Consent Press is a non-profit publisher dedicated to producing affordable, high-quality books that help define and shape the Latter-day Saint experience. BCC Press publishes books that address all aspects of Mormon life. Our mission includes finding manuscripts that will contribute to the lives of thoughtful Latter-day Saints, mentoring authors and nurturing projects to completion, and distributing important books to the Mormon audience at the lowest possible cost.

For information contact
By Common Consent Press
4900 Penrose Dr.
Newburgh, IN 47630

Cover design: D Christian Harrison
Book design: Andrew Heiss

www.bccpress.org

ISBN-978-1-948218-80-1

10 9 8 7 6 5 4 3 2 1

A World of Faith

Second Edition

Text by
Peggy Fletcher Stack

Illustrations by
Kathleen Peterson

BCC PRESS

Preface

Throughout human history, peoples of the world have found deities everywhere.

In the mountains and rivers, suns and moons, stars and oceans, stones by the highway and doves in the air, in chapels and cathedrals, synagogues and sweat lodges, temples and shrines—and in dancing and drumming, praying and pondering, rituals and rhythms, goodness and grandeur.

"Truth is one," says Hinduism's Rig Veda, "but the wise have given it different names."

This children's book celebrates that diversity, offering but a glimpse, a taste, an awakening, an epiphany.

Each page opens with a paragraph about a particular faith's origins. It may be an account of a founder or a shared myth about creation. The second paragraph conveys some of the modern practices of that religious tradition, focusing on infancy, coming of age, worship, and marriage rituals.

We asked members of the faiths or religion scholars to read each page, making sure the explanations are accurate and fair to believers. This is not an academic history, though, but rather summaries in the language of that faith. We wanted kids in each group to recognize themselves and their faith in familiar words.

The religions are organized in alphabetical order and without the number of believers so as not to imply preference. We believe religions should be considered on their merits, not their masses. We have illustrated the faiths with images that are largely historical because current believers tend to dress more alike. An understanding of history is crucial to grasp both the differences and the similarities among religious traditions.

These 32 religious groups are representative, but only a small sample of the world's vast array of believers, followers and practitioners. The first edition in 1998 presumed a mostly American readership and concentrated on the Christian denominations dominating the U.S religious landscape, with a handful of other major faiths, and just one African American group and one African tribe. Now, 25 years later, we are looking at a global audience and have updated the text to be more inclusive and added several traditions—one Asian, two African, two Native American, and one Latin American. We also have examined how some of those Christian groups have expanded.

We have not described in detail the story of Jesus shared by all Christians—that Jesus, a Jew who lived in Jerusalem 2,000 years ago, was the Christ or Son of God and that he was put to death on a cross, but later was resurrected, and that his followers launched a movement based on his teaching—because we are intrigued by the ways in which each group's understanding of those events may be a bit different from the rest. For Hindu, Buddhist, Jewish, Muslim and other believers, the divisions within their traditions also tell a story.

Summarizing centuries-old religions in a single page has been daunting and nearly impossible. But doing it has shown us clearly what they all have in common: a sense of otherworldliness, a hunger for practicing greater love and compassion to their neighbors, and a way to express their values in ritual.

Bigotry begins with ignorance, and many children—no matter what country—know little to nothing about faiths other than their own. We hope these pages will show them unexpected parallels today so they can be peacemakers tomorrow.

The National Cathedral in Washington, D.C.; the compass rose is the symbol of
the Anglican Communion; the Episcopal shield represents the old church and new
church; the scallop shell symbolizes baptism; gold rings suggest the Trinity.

Anglican

Legend has it that Joseph of Arimathea, the man who provided a tomb for Jesus, traveled to England and planted a sprig from Christ's crown of thorns. The prickly tree slowly flowered there, and so did Christianity. For hundreds of years, England was a Christian and Catholic nation. By the sixteenth century, though, tensions between King Henry VIII of England and the Catholic pope boiled over. They argued about marriage laws, church property, and who would govern the church. Finally, Henry said that the British kings or queens would be the "Supreme Head" of the Church of England and would choose its clergy. At the end of the American Revolution, the colonists from England established their own bishops. While maintaining ties to England, American members eventually became known as Episcopalians, from the Greek word "episkopos," meaning bishop.

Anglicans praise God with magnificent music, ritual reverence, and exalted awe. Their British ancestors built stately cathedrals and produced two of the most majestic books in the English language: the King James translation of the Bible and the *Book of Common Prayer*, which contains readings still used in worship. Like Catholics, Lutherans, and Eastern Orthodox, Anglicans believe in Christ's real presence at the Lord's Supper. They baptize infants and adults by pouring, sprinkling, or immersing them in water. The U.S. Episcopal church is still connected to the Church of England, which has branches on every continent. Together, the churches form the Anglican Communion, which strives to follow Christ in his suffering, forgiveness, and compassion.

The Shrine of the Báb at Mt. Carmel, Haifa, Israel; hands symbolize prayer; the dove means peace; the nine-pointed star represents the unity of all religions; the three-tiered symbol represents God, the holy messengers, and humanity.

Baha'i

In 1844 a man called the Báb, which means "gate," announced to the people of Persia (now Iran) that a messenger of God was coming soon. The Báb said that this new prophet would bring peace to all the world. But the people were afraid of the Báb. They thought he was rebelling against the government, so they killed him. A few years later a young man came forward to say that he was the messenger that the Báb had foretold. The young man was called Baha'u'llah, or "Glory of God." He taught the people that God had sent many prophets to this world at different times. God is one and all religions have truth, he said. The peoples of the earth are like fragrant, multicolored blossoms in a heavenly garden. Baha'u'llah was tortured and imprisoned for these beliefs.

Baha'is revere Baha'u'llah as the divine teacher for this day. They have no priests or clergy, but each group is led by a nine-member spiritual assembly. They pray three times a day. Every nineteen days they hold a feast to pray, enjoy each other's company, and remember events in their history. Baha'i children study world religions and Baha'i houses of worship have nine sides and nine doors to symbolize the many paths to God, who is continuously revealed to humanity. But most of all, Baha'is teach world peace and unity through understanding and obedience to the laws of God.

First Baptist church, built in 1774 in Providence, Rhode Island; Greek letters on the book are alpha and omega, the beginning and the end; the dove means the Holy Spirit; in the corner is the symbol of American Baptists.

Baptist

Some English-speaking Christians in seventeenth-century Europe taught, like Martin Luther, that believers should read and interpret the Bible for themselves and that baptism should be an adult decision. Roger Williams was one of them. He was an independent Englishman who insisted on worshipping God in his own way and who sailed to America in 1631 to get away from the state-sponsored religion back home. Arriving in Massachusetts, he discovered the Puritans had established an official church and demanded strict obedience to it. When Williams complained to the leaders, saying that people should be able to follow their individual consciences, they forced him to leave. He fled into the wilderness during the coldest snows of winter. Finally, Williams settled in Rhode Island and declared that the people of this colony would be allowed to choose their own religion. His was the first Baptist church in America.

Baptists worldwide reject the idea of infant baptism, saying that people must understand Christ's gospel before they take that step. Though believers are typically immersed in water like the biblical John the Baptist, it is a symbolic act, not a sacrament, an outward expression of an inward transformation. Today's Baptists celebrate the Lord's Supper at least four times a year. They revere the Bible as the inspired word of God. Each Baptist church is independent of all the other ones, though some churches unite for common missions. Baptists across the world, including in countries like Burma (now Myanmar), have a passion for "soul freedom" or finding their own path to God.

The Bodhnath Stupa in Kathmandu, Nepal; a prayer wheel, bodhi tree, and lotus flower, which symbolize remaining clean in a muddy pond. The wheel of truth in the corner has eight spokes representing the eightfold path.

Buddhist

In about 536 B.C.E. Siddhartha Gautama, a 30-year-old prince in India, left his home in search of wisdom. He spent six years living in a forest and listening to religious teachers. But he was not satisfied. Finally one day he sat under a bodhi (fig) tree, where he decided to stay until he received some answers. By morning his mind was opened to a vision of life's deeper meaning and to his previous lives. According to tradition, that was the day Siddhartha became the Buddha, which means "the enlightened one."

Life is mostly suffering that comes from wanting things, says the Buddha. These desires can be overcome by following an eightfold path called the Middle Way, which avoids extremes. Buddhists believe in treating all living things with respect, speaking honestly, helping others, and learning to focus the mind. Those who follow this path will understand the truths of the universe. They believe there is no individual soul or self. Instead, people are reincarnated, or born at different times, again and again until they reach Nirvana (perfect unity with the divine), and are freed from the cycle. Buddhism is practiced primarily in Thailand, Nepal, Japan, Korea, China and throughout Asia. In some countries, Buddhist men and women become monks and nuns who wear simple orange robes, eat only one meal a day, live together in communities, and never marry. All Buddhists seek enlightenment like the Buddha.

Chartres Cathedral in France; a young girl's first Communion; the cross is a symbol of the crucifixion of Jesus Christ; rosary beads are used to help with prayers; a paschal candle is used especially at Easter.

Catholic

In the Bible it says that Jesus of Nazareth could heal the sick and raise the dead. People followed him everywhere to hear his teachings. During his ministry, Jesus chose twelve disciples to be his apostles. One of them, a fisherman named Peter, became their leader. For Roman Catholics, Peter was the first pope. Throughout the ages, popes and other church leaders have explained Jesus' life and teachings and spread the good news of the Christian gospel across the planet from east to west and north to south.

Catholics believe the word of God is found in the Bible and in church teachings and practices. Special ceremonies called "sacraments" are at the heart of Catholic life and are ways in which God's saving love is expressed through the church. Some sacraments are celebrated at important moments like birth, becoming mature, marriage, and death. Other sacraments such as confessing of sins and participating in the Mass (commemorating the Lord's Supper) occur more often. In the Mass, Catholics believe the bread and wine are mysteriously transformed into the body and blood of Christ. Catholics revere Jesus' mother, Mary, as both a saint and as the Mother of God. Saints are people who were especially close to God in this life; from heaven they help the living. Priests and nuns are men and women who remain single in order to better serve God and the church. For Catholics, God is present and active in every experience of life.

T'ien Tan (part of the Temple of Heaven in Beijing, China, built in 1420); the crane is a symbol of strength and longevity; the border letters symbolize the teachings of Confucius.

Confucian

Confucius was a Chinese scholar, born in 551 B.C.E, who felt that the people of his time had forgotten the way to behave. Local rulers fought with each other, while being greedy and creating chaos. Confucius studied past civilizations and then traveled the countryside for 13 years trying to persuade those rulers to listen to his ideas. When that didn't work, he turned to his students, sharing what he learned—that people should to be kind to their neighbors, to honor their parents and ancestors, respect their leaders, and hold their tempers. He believed that everyone, rich and poor, should be educated in history, music, poetry, and more. These principles, though simple, had a powerful effect on people in China. After Confucius died, his followers compiled his sayings into a book, the Analects, to be studied and even memorized. Eventually, those who embraced Confucian concepts built temples to honor him, and his ideas were adopted as the organizing principles for the Chinese nation, while spreading to Japan, Korea, and Vietnam.

Today, many people in these parts of Asia still follow Confucius's teachings, learning the basics of good behavior and thinking. In these places, some hold ceremonies to mark important times in life such as reaching adulthood, getting married, or passing away. Many practitioners go to Confucian temples to pray for help with their studies or remember their ancestors with a home shrine. To the followers of Confucius, the chief human virtues are compassion, thoughtfulness, righteousness, wisdom, trust, generosity, endurance, and unselfishness—all to build a just and good society.

Mount Taishan is the most famous mountain shrine in China; the eight trigrams are used with the Daoist writings; the five elements or forces of nature are suggested by different colors: fire is red, water is black, earth is yellow; wood is green, and metal is white.

Daoist

It is said that Laozi, a Chinese bookkeeper, was disgusted with the foolishness at the ruler's court around the sixth century B.C.E. and left for the countryside. As he reached the city's gates, a guard begged Laozi to tell all that he had learned. His words became the Dao De Jing, a book about the "Dao" or the way the world goes through creative transformations. The Dao was associated with the terms "yin" and "yang," which represented fluctuating forces, including life and death, day and night, as well as male and female powers. These forces are not polar opposites but merge and separate, creating life's many rhythms.

Daoists still believe the world is populated with many spirits. In Daoist temples, priests communicate with these spirits for people who want to be healed, purified, and find the help they need. These priests also perform offerings to aid seekers in gaining insight for their lives. Individual practitioners who strive to follow the Dao believe that all things are made of "qi," or the vital energy that ranges from heavy (yin) to light (yang). To live a long and healthy life, they work to ensure their qi is constantly balanced. This is done by breathing and other physical exercises that enable the qi to cycle properly through the body. By understanding life's ups and downs, the Dao allows people to attain a higher form of joy.

The Hagia Sophia in Istanbul, Turkey; candles symbolize the light of Christ's gospel; the crown symbolizes the triumph of Jesus over death.

Eastern Orthodox

On the eve of a battle in 312 C.E. for control of the Roman Empire, Constantine the Great saw a flaming cross symbolizing Jesus Christ in the sky and the words, "With this sign, conquer." After his victory, Constantine took that as a sign and converted to Christianity, which eventually became the empire's official religion. He moved the capital eastward to Constantinople (today's Istanbul in Turkey). But Christians in the Eastern Roman Empire argued with those in the West over the exact relationship between God, Jesus, and the Holy Spirit. They also disagreed about whether the pope was the supreme head of the church or just one bishop among many, on the language of worship, and how to visually depict holy figures (two-dimensional or full figured). By 1054, a split in the church, which came to be known as "the Great Schism," was unavoidable. The Greek-speakers in the East became Eastern Orthodox (meaning "right belief") and those in the West, who favored Latin, were known as Roman Catholics.

The Eastern Orthodox church, which is organized by regions such as Greece, Serbia, Ukraine or Russia, shares many beliefs and practices with the Roman Catholic church including ceremonies known as sacraments. But in the Orthodox church, infants are baptized by immersion and some priests can marry. In the church's colorful wedding ceremony, the bride and groom wear crowns symbolizing their new joy in marriage and Christ. Orthodox believers use icons, or ornate, two-dimensional paintings of biblical figures and saints, which are seen as "windows to the kingdom of God," to help them express their love of God. It is a faith steeped in mystery and beauty.

Rajgopuram, the Hindu Temple of Greater Chicago; the word "OM" expresses the complete nature of God; the gods Krishna, Rama, and Ganesh are in the border; fruit, incense, and candles are offerings to the gods; cows represent four paths to union with God.

Hindu

Over five thousand years ago, some wandering tribes settled on the banks of the Indus River (in modern-day India) and told stories of the many gods who ruled over fire, water, rain and rivers. They talked about a god named Vishnu who came to earth in different forms (avatars) to help humanity. Once he was a giant fish warning of a dangerous flood. Another time he was a tortoise churning an elixir of immortality. One of the avatars was Rama, a prince who had to fight a multi-headed demon to rescue his kidnapped wife. Another was Krishna, a wise chariot driver who served others in battle. At the same time, Lakshmi was revered as the goddess and giver of prosperity, and Durga as mother to all creation. All these gods are aspects of one Brahman, the supreme spirit of the universe that has no beginning or end.

According to their holy books of knowledge, the Vedas, Hindus believe that human souls are born over and over into different circumstances until they reach perfection or union with God. For them, every action has a consequence in this life or the next, called the law of karma. Bad actions can lead to a new life full of suffering; good choices may be rewarded with good fortune. They teach that humans have four goals: acquire wealth, enjoy love, fulfill one's duty, and attain wisdom. Most Hindu homes throughout the world have a family shrine where the faithful light a lamp and pray every day. Because all living creatures, including cows, are revered as sacred, some Hindus will not eat meat. Devotion, meditation, and colorful festivals can open their minds and hearts to God. For them, religion ("dharma") is the vision of life that combines the spiritual with the material.

A Hopi pueblo in Mesa Verde, Colorado; the four colors of corn—red, black, yellow, and white—represent brotherhood; the eagle feathers symbolize power

Hopi

In the beginning, say the Hopis, human beings lived underground, far below the surface of the earth. But they were crowded and constantly tripping over each other. So they made their way up through three different worlds until they found a hole in the earth's surface. They climbed through the hole to see the sky and breathe the air. This was the Fourth World, where they met Maasaw, creator and caretaker god, who told the humans that this world is not as easy as the other three. It has height and depth, heat and cold, beauty and emptiness. Humans promised they would care for the Earth. Then Maasaw departed, leaving them with ancestral spirits or "kachinas" to guide them on their journey.

Hopis, referred to as "peaceful people," are among the Pueblo Indians of the American West. They believe that people have bodies, minds and spirits and health comes from maintaining a balance in the three. To Hopis, who were farmers, corn is a symbol of life. When Hopi babies are born, they are given a special blanket and a perfect ear of corn. Kachinas bring rain, heal the sick, and help crops grow. They hold ceremonies in underground chambers called "kivas," where a small hole in the corner represents the place humans entered the world. Dancers dressed as individual kachinas, with painted bodies and colorful masks to represent a particular spiritual essence, call on the spirits to bless these homes with good fortune and protect against evil. In their beliefs and rituals, Hopis celebrate all of God's creations and try to keep harmony in the universe.

Jain temple in Nairobi, Kenya; Kshamavani Parva Festival in India; Jain priests and nuns. Border: Swastika represents four states of existence; Om symbol; hand is a gesture of blessing; Jain flag colors represent the five vows.

Jain

In the sixth century B.C.E., around the same time as Siddhartha (eventually the Buddha) was seeking enlightenment, another Indian prince, Nataputta Mahavira, was looking for a way to escape the endless cycle of death and rebirth. Mahavira left his home in an eastern Indian palace and met up with a group of monks, who followed the philosophy of a long-dead teacher named Parshva. Then Mahavira wandered naked through the villages of northern India, believing that he needed to rid himself of all belongings—including gold and silver, horses and chariots, and even clothing—and to avoid killing any living creature. He sometimes used a broom to sweep his path of any insects he might unknowingly crush. After 12 years of practicing extreme self-discipline and denial, Mahavira achieved liberation from reincarnation and became known as the "Jina" or spiritual conqueror.

Jains believe in higher beings called "devas," but not in a creator god. It is up to each person to free themselves to find multiple lives by living a moral life. They take five vows—to be non-violent (a principle known as "ahimsa"), truthful, celibate, and not to steal or become attached to possessions. Jains believe all living things, including animals, plants and insects, have a right to exist, so many wear cloth over their mouths to prevent accidentally swallowing a bug. Jains attempt to master their experience through the jewels of faith, knowledge and action.

World Headquarters in Brooklyn, New York; the watchtower symbolizes the need to watch for the return of Jesus; every member is a missionary.

Jehovah's Witnesses

The late 1880s were tough times in America. Workers were fighting with their bosses, people were getting poorer, and the world was getting ready for war. Charles Taze Russell was convinced that Jesus was coming soon. He believed that there would be a big battle in which the wicked would be destroyed forever and the righteous would rule the world for 1,000 years. By 1931, many people agreed with him. They established the Watch Tower Bible and Tract Society in Brooklyn, New York, and called themselves Jehovah's Witnesses. Witnesses were often persecuted for their devotion to God above country and for their refusal to salute flags or serve in the military. In America they eventually won the right to practice their religion in their own way.

Witnesses believe that God—known as Jehovah, a name derived from Hebrew—once existed alone. Jesus was Jehovah's first creation as a spirit son. He was born a man and then became man's savior by his perfect obedience. Every Jehovah's Witness endeavors to preach the faith's message through the church magazine, *The Watchtower*, for at least ten hours a month. Witnesses don't celebrate Christmas or Easter. Instead, they commemorate what they believe is the biblical anniversary of Christ's death. Baptism is their only other religious ceremony. They wait faithfully for Christ's return.

Bouwmeesterstraat Synagogue in Antwerp, Belgium; the Star of David; the menorah, the oldest symbol of Judaism; the writing says, "Hear, O Israel, the Lord is our God, the Lord is one."

Jewish

In the ancient land of Canaan near the Mediterranean Sea lived a man named Abraham. He was a good and noble man who believed in one God. But his neighbors worshipped many gods, even gods made of bronze. Abraham's God made a promise to him. If he were devoted only to God and obeyed God's rules, that divine being would bless Abraham and all his children for many generations to come. God would give them a special land and protect them from their enemies. Jews get their name from Judah, a great-grandson of Abraham.

Jews read, study, and revere the words of their ancient prophets and leaders which are written in the Torah—the first five books of the Bible. It has stories of the first human couple, Adam and Eve, in the Garden of Eden, as well as morality tales of Noah and the flood, Moses leading the Israelites out of Egypt, Esther protecting her people, David killing the giant Goliath, and Joshua with his mighty trumpet. The Torah also sets out the rules and rituals of a righteous life, including the Ten Commandments. Jews observe a weekly day of rest, or sabbath, from sundown Friday until sundown Saturday. When Jewish boys are thirteen, they read from the Torah in Hebrew at a synagogue service called a "bar mitzvah." By doing this, they become members of the congregation. In some groups girls have the same ceremony, called a "bat mitzvah." Jews celebrate God's past and present miracles with holidays throughout the year, and they strive to be faithful to Abraham's promises to God.

Sweat lodge; Sundance Tree; Medicine Wheel represents man's sacred path through life. Colors: white (north) purity, cleansing, health; yellow (east) inspiration, beginning light; red (south) growth, change, family nourishment; black (west) introspection, insight, power. Border: eagle and hawk feathers; sun; Lakota symbol represents the relationship of Native Americans with the universe (lower triangle pointing up represents earth while the top triangle pointing down represents stars and sun).

Lakota

Long ago, during a time of famine in American buffalo country, two scouts went looking for food and saw a white cloud coming over the hills. As it got closer, the shape of a beautiful woman emerged—a spirit woman. Treating the exquisite personage as nothing but a potential wife, the first man was enveloped into the mist and became a pile of bones. The mysterious spirit instructed the other one to tell his Lakota people to pitch their tents in a circle, making a large tipi in the center, and she would bestow a great gift upon them. When the spirit figure (who became known as White Buffalo Calf Woman) arrived, she gave the leader a small pipe made of red stone to be used in ceremonies to heal mind, body, and spirit.

Lakotas, who live in the open plains of North and South Dakota in the United States, observe these seven rites: Keeping of the Soul (a lock of the deceased's hair for a year): Purifying the Soul (through sweat lodges), Crying for a Vision (communicating with spirits through a guide), Making Relatives (building commonality with other tribes), Coming of Age (preparing for womanhood), Throwing of the Ball (showing unity with the Earth), and the most important rite of all, the Sun Dance, in which dancers circle a tree to learn bravery, endurance and sacrifice, while connecting to the universe and beyond. They remain true to what White Buffalo Calf Woman taught, with their sacred pipe always beside them.

Seneca people; Medicine Wheel: white (north) winter, death, white-skinned people, intellect / mind; yellow (east) spring, birth, yellow-skinned people, sun, dawn,
growth, emotional heart / fire; red (south) summer, youth, red-skinned people,
moon, water, spiritual / soul; black (west) autumn, adult, black-skinned people,
maturity, dusk, physical / body. Border: turtle, hawk feathers, beans, corn, squash.

Longhouse

As he lay dying in 1799 of a frightful disease, a Seneca Indian chief, healer, and prophet in western New York had a vision of three spirit messengers. These heavenly visitors told Ganioda'yo ("Handsome Lake") to spread the Gai'wiio, or "good word," to his people. They should give up drunkenness, laziness, witchcraft, and mistreating women and children. Instead, they needed to be sober, industrious, faithful to their spouses, and treat everyone with compassion. Handsome Lake urged his listeners among the Six Nations of the Iroqois to cultivate and harvest crops, to raise horses and cattle, to go to school, to live a godly life, and to glorify the Creator. After the dream, children gathered around him, so he could embrace them and share his newfound wisdom.

His words were passed down as "The Code of Handsome Lake," which combined traditions from the Iroqois nation with some aboriginal and Christian values. Today, followers in Canada and the northeastern United States gather by a fireplace in historic longhouses during Green Corn festivals in late August and Winter festivals to hear the code recited from memory by preachers. It is a time of confession, casting out evil, mourning for the dead, and giving thanks to the Great Spirit—all due to the miraculous vision of one man.

St. John's Evangelical Lutheran church in Salt Lake City; Martin Luther's coat of arms; the Luther rose; the Christian heart rests on roses beneath the cross; the dove means the Holy Spirit; Luther is in the lower right-hand corner.

Lutheran

Martin Luther, a Catholic priest in sixteenth-century Germany, spent a lot of time wondering if he was pleasing God. He was frustrated with his own failure to be free of sinfulness. He was also troubled by some of the church's practices—including "indulgences" to reduce a person's time in purgatory—that were not biblical. They were wrong, Luther declared. He made a list of 95 complaints and nailed them to a castle door in Wittenberg. Though Luther only meant to reform the Catholic church, his actions launched the Protestant Reformation and divided Christians into many different groups.

People do not need priests to understand the Bible, Luther taught; they can study it themselves. To make it easier for common folks, he translated the Bible from Latin into German. All believers are priests, he said. But no matter how hard people try to be good, everyone sins. Only faith in Jesus Christ and repentance will lead a person to heaven. Holy lives are built upon faith, not actions. Lutherans baptize infants by sprinkling or pouring water onto their foreheads. They celebrate the Lord's Supper each week, believing—like Catholics, Episcopalians, and Eastern Orthodox—that Christ is truly present in the bread and wine. And once a year on Reformation Sunday, Lutherans remember the grace-filled courage of their founder.

A typical camp meeting and circuit rider; the cross and flame symbolize zeal to preach the gospel; the triangle suggests the Trinity; the cross and rings represent marriage; the fish is the symbol of Jesus Christ; IHS means Jesus in Greek.

Methodist

John Wesley, an eighteenth-century priest in the Church of England, believed it was important to strive for perfection. He planned every minute of his time to study, pray, or discuss religious ideas. Wesley's fellow students called him and his friends "Methodists" because they were so methodical or orderly. Years later Wesley had a sudden, inner feeling that Christ loved him. He started preaching in open fields. His brother Charles wrote more than 6,000 hymns to be sung during these outdoor meetings. During the American Revolution, Methodist societies in the United States broke off from the Church of England and formed a church of their own. On the western frontier, Methodist ministers became "circuit-riders," traveling from place to place, holding services in large tents, and preaching to thousands day and night.

Methodists internationally still push for perfection in themselves and the world around them. They fight for justice and peace, while caring for the poor and hungry—and they believe God is helping them, encouraging them, and showing the way. Like Catholics, they baptize infants. For Methodists, the Bible is the inspired word of God, and all people must read and understand it for themselves. Methodists celebrate the Lord's Supper often. And they love the joyous singing of hymns—many composed by Charles Wesley.

The LDS temple in Salt Lake City, Utah; sego lilies are the state flowers of Utah; the sun, moon, and stars represent three tiers of heaven; the beehives suggest industry; the angels sounding the word of God, the all-seeing eye, and the words "Holiness to the Lord" appear on the temple.

Mormon

In 1820, a 14-year-old farm boy, Joseph Smith Jr., told his family and neighbors that he had seen a vision of God and Jesus Christ while praying in the New York woods. These other-worldly visitors told him that precious truths of Christianity had been lost but would be restored. Some years later, Smith was led by an angel to gold plates buried in the ground. The plates told the story of Christ's visit to a group of ancient Israelites who had sailed to the Americas. With God's help, Smith translated the record called the Book of Mormon. These believers, dubbed Mormons, embraced it as scripture, along with the Bible. Smith founded The Church of Jesus Christ of Latter-day Saints in 1830, but many other Christians believed that Mormons were wrong. They drove these young believers from state to state until Smith was killed by a mob in 1844. Brigham Young, who became the church's next president, led the beleaguered believers to the mountains of Utah, where they established the "Beehive State."

Mormons, (who now prefer to be called Latter-day Saints) most of whom now live outside the United States, follow some traditional Christian practices such as a weekly Lord's Supper (which they call "the sacrament" and which includes bread and water) and baptism by immersion. But they also have special ceremonies in temples where believers are baptized by proxy for their ancestors and where families are united for eternity. The church is led by a man they consider to be a prophet, along with twelve apostles; local leaders are drawn from congregations to serve without pay for a limited period of time. The church sends missionaries two by two all over the world to preach their restored Christianity and to assure their listeners they can get back to God.

The Masjid Jamek, in Kuala Lumpur, Malaysia; the decorative writing in the background is from the Qu'ran: O, Lord, we only worship thee and thus seek your guidance and help." The writing to the right says, "I begin with the name of my Lord most merciful and beneficent," and in the border, "I seek protection from my creator against Satan the Cursed."

Muslim

When the prophet Abraham and his wife Sarah could not have children, God told Abraham to marry Sarah's companion, Hagar, as his second wife. She had a son, Ishmael. Later, God commanded Abraham to take Hagar and her baby to the desert and leave them there. Abraham obeyed. In the barren landscape, Hagar ran from one hill to another seven times looking for water, while Ishmael cried and kicked the ground. According to tradition, water suddenly sprung up where the baby's feet had scraped the sand. The miraculous well became a hallowed spot (now Zamzam Springs) and later part of the city of Makkah (Mecca). It is near where Muslims believe that Abraham and Ishmael built the first pilgrim shrine to God, known as the Ka'bah. Centuries later, Muhammad, a merchant in Makkah, was troubled by the worship of idols. He spent hours praying in a cave until the Angel Gabriel appeared to him with the message that there is only one Creator God, called "Allah" in Arabic. Then the angel dictated to Muhammad other principles to share with the world.

Those who believe in one God and in Muhammad as his last prophet are called Muslims, and their religion is Islam, which means "peaceful submission" to God. The divine revelations to the prophet were recorded and together constitute the Qu'ran, Islam's scripture. Muslims pray at least five times a day. They give to the poor, fast from sunrise to sunset during the month of Ramadan, and they travel to Makkah at least once in their lives to encircle the shrine of Abraham. Muslims believe that, if they fulfill these duties faithfully, they will have walked a straight and holy path.

Nuer people; cattle serve as companions and define lifestyle. Border: sun, moon are signs of God; rainbow is God's necklace; rain, lightning, thunder represent coming of God; spear; Nuer flag—red, white, black, green.

Nuer

Long ago, Nuer elders, living along the swampy flood plains and open sa-vannas of the White Nile, taught that their ancestors descended from the sky by climbing down a sacred samerind tree to Earth. The Nuer raised cattle and honored the divine creator, Kuoth Nhia ("God of the Sky"), as well as lesser spirits, who brought life and health, with rites and offer-ings. Some of their priests were seen as mystical intermediaries between mortals and divinities of the earth and sky. Some feared the "evil eye," or witches who had supernatural power to curse them with a single look.

Cattle herding remains central to the religious life of the Nuer liv-ing and worshipping in what is now South Sudan. They also have elabo-rate coming-of-age and marriage ceremonies. They believe living beings possess three elements: flesh, breath, and legacy. Though they have no concept of an afterlife, they do believe that their dead ancestors can bless or curse them. They can contact those spirits by dedicating and naming cows for their ancestors and then rubbing the animals with ashes in a solemn ritual. Young men make six cuts in their forehead to signify that they have reached adulthood, should not be afraid, and will live honor-ably. After marriage, the husband's family does not believe that a mar-riage was a good match until the wife has her third child. Together, the Nuer people look for signs of God in the sky, the clouds, the lightning and the rain.

Wedding ceremony; shamans making offerings of food and coca leaves to Pachamama (give back what is taken); llamas. Border: symbols of water, sun, earth, moon (four Quechua principles claim Pachamama origin).

Pachamama

To the ancient Incas of South America's Andes mountains, the supreme deity was female—Pachamama or Earth Mother. As a figure of generosity and abundance, she governed nature and its fertility rhythms from planting to harvest. She was also a protector of Earth's inhabitants and expected that they would give back to her offerings of grain, potatoes, coca leaves, and seeds. It was a reciprocal relationship, symbolizing balance between the spiritual and physical worlds. However, this goddess also was believed to cause earthquakes.

Today, many indigenous peoples in Argentina, Bolivia, Chile, Ecuador, and Peru spend the entire month of August celebrating Pachamama in their own way. In Peru, some decorate their houses with yellow petals or confetti and light incense in every room to cleanse them of evil spirits. In Argentina, participants dig a hole outside their homes, representing the "mouth of the Earth," and fill it with red and white flower petals, candy, rice, anise, beans and peanuts, llama fat and wine. Women weave fibers of red, green, yellow and blue into Andean sacred blankets for use in the consecration ceremony. Others hold their offerings to the sky and shout prayers of praise and gratitude. They believe the Earth Mother, who embodies the mountains, has showered them in their dry and harsh landscape with her bounteous goodness.

The flying dove and the fire represent the Holy Spirit; the cross symbolizes Jesus' death; the fish represents Christ.

Pentecostal

One foggy evening in the spring of 1906, a group of Christians met in a Los Angeles warehouse to praise God and pray. As Reverend William J. Seymour was preaching, strange, unfamiliar sounds came out of his mouth. The one-eyed, Black pastor from Texas was "speaking in tongues"—a sort of divine language. His body was shaking with the power of the new sounds. Soon, other people were doing the same thing. The whole building seemed to rock. Every day for the next three years, from early morning until midnight, thousands flocked to the warehouse on Azusa Street seeking the Holy Spirit. With that revival, Pentecostalism, a charismatic Christian movement, had begun. Over the next hundred years, it would sweep across North and South America, across to Africa and up to Asia. With no central hierarchy, it often attracted impoverished or marginalized believers.

"Pentecost" means fifty and refers to an event described in the New Testament held fifty days after Passover, when 120 of Jesus' disciples and other followers met together and were filled with the Holy Spirit. Pentecostals believe that each Christian can experience baptism by the Holy Spirit like the disciples. They believe that God still miraculously heals today. In Sunday services, many believers worship with arms raised above their heads, as a sign of surrender to God, as a child raising arms to an earthly father. Sometimes the languages they speak are not understandable to others, but are a real verbal expression of love to the Father through the Holy Spirit. Pentecostals seek complete openness to an outpouring of God's spirit.

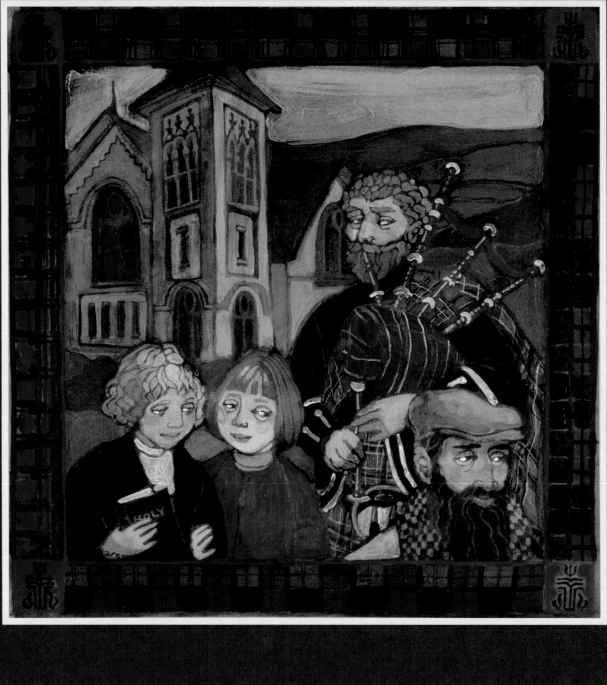

The Third Presbyterian Church in Salt Lake City, Utah; the tartan plaids of Scotland remind people of the church's beginnings; the symbol of the Presbyterian Church (USA) is in the corners.

Presbyterian

John Calvin, a forceful and renowned sixteenth-century French-Swiss theologian, thought of God as the supreme ruler—wise, powerful, and loving. This mighty God knows all things, including who is saved, Calvin taught, and his will is expressed in the scriptures. Calvin rejected all Catholic traditions that were not mentioned in the Bible—saints, pilgrimages, and certain prayers. He believed that churches should be led not by a pope or bishop but by a group of church members known as "presbyters," or elders. John Knox, a devout follower of Calvin, brought Calvin's ideas to Scotland, where the Parliament declared Presbyterianism the state religion in 1560.

When they came to America, Presbyterians were among the strongest supporters of the Revolutionary War. King George of England famously called the war a "Presbyterian Rebellion." Their form of church government influenced the new country's ideas of democracy. They believed that everyone should have a say in governing church and country. Because they believed strongly in learning, they established more than seventy colleges and universities, including Princeton. Like many other Protestants, Presbyterians baptize infants and celebrate the Lord's Supper monthly. Some missionaries have shared the good news of Jesus across the globe, including in South Korea, where about half of all Christians are Presbyterians. God rules the universe, they assert, with all the faithful as his humble and equal servants.

A Friends' meetinghouse in Birmingham, Pennsylvania, in 1763; the candle represents the inner light in each person; the star is the black and red star of the American Friends' Service; George Fox is in the center of the illustration.

Quaker

George Fox felt he could not find truth in the seventeenth-century English churches. The sermons and the ceremonies were not enough for him. While praying one day, he heard a voice tell him that Truth is inside every human being. This Inner Light can be reached through prayer and meditation. With this new insight, Fox preached equality between men and women, rich and poor, slave and free. Fox refused to take off his hat to royalty or to support clergy. Though they called themselves "The Religious Society of Friends," Fox's followers were nicknamed Quakers for saying that human beings would tremble—or quake—in God's presence. The Quakers were constantly persecuted—several were even hanged—before they found havens in some U.S. states.

Quakers oppose war and shun oaths. Their churches are simple, without paintings or organs or pulpits. During services, believers wait in silence until the Holy Spirit moves them to speak. Many congregations, called "meetings," have no paid clergy because they believe that all members are ministers. No special ceremonies such as baptism or the Lord's Supper are used. With small congregations throughout the United States, Europe, Scandinavia, Russia and Africa, Quakers cherish the Bible for its truth, but they also believe that God communicates with human beings through divine revelation or the Inner Light.

A corps building in Dawson City, British Columbia, Canada, built in 1900; the shield suggests protection against sin; the crest says "blood and fire" to preach the gospel.

Salvation Army

William Booth was leading a Christian mission among London's poor in the 1860s and feeling discouraged. Faith was not enough, he felt. His converts needed to get to work. But what would rally them? One day a church member called the group "God's volunteer army." Booth replied, "We're not volunteers. We are always on duty." In that moment, he decided to rename the mission "the Salvation Army." Almost immediately, the group came alive. Modeled after the military, ministers became officers, congregations were corps, and members were transformed into soldiers. They donned uniforms, took up bugles, and marched against hunger and suffering with the motto: "Soap, soup, and salvation."

Salvationists, with headquarters still in England, meet for weekly devotionals in any available structure. Officer (minister) candidates, both men and women, must be between eighteen and thirty-five years old with at least two years of formal Bible study. Men and women have been equal partners in leading the Army since it began. Uniformed officers can often be seen on street corners at Christmas carrying red kettles and ringing bells while collecting money for the poor. Sin destroys the soul and the society, they believe. But Jesus—with the help of the Army—can save everyone.

An Adventist church in Jackson, Mississippi; the fruits, vegetables, and grains represent the ethic of health; the three angels symbolize the second coming of Jesus; Ellen White is seen in the lower right.

Seventh-day Adventist

On the evening of October 22, 1844, seventeen-year-old Ellen White was among thousands of people waiting on rooftops and in churches to see Jesus. William Miller, a farmer who had studied the Bible, predicted that it would be the day of Christ's second coming. When nothing happened, most people went home, calling the day "the Great Disappointment." Ellen, a frail young girl, continued to meet with a small group of people who were trying to understand what went wrong. They concluded that, instead of coming to Earth, Christ had moved into the Most Holy Place in heaven for the next stage of his ministry. This was the beginning of the world's preparations for Jesus, and Ellen was to be one of God's messengers.

The name "Seventh-day Adventist" contains two of the church's beliefs. The word "advent" means "to come" and refers to Christ's return; the "seventh day," or Saturday, is when they celebrate the sabbath, instead of Sunday. Adventists emphasize good health and do not drink alcohol or smoke, and many are vegetarians. They believe in baptism by immersion for those who have reached an understanding of their commitment to Christ. Adventists, with large congregations in Africa, Asia and Latin America, educate their youth in their own schools, build hospitals for the needy, and send out missionaries from their U.S. headquarters to prepare the world for the Second Coming.

The torii, or gateway to the sacred space (two columns crossed by two beams). Mt. Fuji, Japan, is in the background; the sun represents the beginning of life in Japan; the thick rope of shimenawa suggests the sacred; the length of folded paper is the resting place of gods during prayer.

Shinto

The world was once a great cloud of chaos. Slowly, there emerged spirits called "kami," or gods, including the powerful sun goddess Amaterasu (or "heaven illuminating god"). When treated with care and respect, kami bless human lives, they believed, but if ignored or mistreated, the same gods become harmful monsters. So people made offerings to the gods in exchange for their help against disaster and suffering. Japan means the "origin of the sun," and Shinto followers in that island nation see their emperor or empress as mythical descendants from the Sun Goddess.

Shinto—the way of the gods—teaches followers that the gods are everywhere. At shrines, priests perform rituals on behalf of believers seeking good fortune, health and prosperity. Their torii (gates) divide the secular from the sacred. But even trees, rocks, and waterfalls can be home to kami. Their presence is marked by ropes with paper tassels. Believers also can worship kami at home with food offerings such as rice, salt, and wine, or on the mountainside. There are Shinto ceremonies for certain times of life: birth, growing up, and marriage, as well as for the harvest, which often includes cleansing rituals. At numerous all-day festivals throughout the islands, people celebrate together. Often a small portable shrine containing neighborhood kami is carried on the shoulders of young men, passing by to bless their households. Shinto beliefs help people of Japan stay focused on the present moment, on the power that all things have. A clean, often-washed heart can feel that power.

The Golden Temple in the Pool of Immortality in Amritsar, India; a sword is one of the five symbols of Sikh faith; the diamond pattern imitates the tiles of the plaza.

Sikh

In northern India during the late fifteenth century, a young man named Guru Nanak was troubled by the fighting he saw in neighboring countries between Muslims, who believed in one God, and Hindus, who taught that God takes many forms. While pondering these claims, Nanak disappeared and didn't return for three days. He was summoned into God's presence, Sikhs believe, where he learned that there is only one truth: universal love. Nanak's insight was passed down through the generations by nine successive gurus, or spiritual leaders and teachers. Two hundred years after Nanak, Guru Gobind Singh directed the Sikhs—meaning disciples—to form a society of holy men and soldiers to defend their faith. This group, called Khalsa, developed five outward signs of their loyalty: uncut hair covered with a turban, a comb to hold the hair, a dagger, a steel wristband, and short trousers. Soon all male Sikhs adopted the signs. Later, females were invited to join the Khalsa.

God is not revealed in religious ceremonies, but in quiet prayer and with the help of gurus, say the Sikhs. God himself is a guru. Sikhs say five different prayers a day, each one written by a different guru. Boys and girls become members of the Khalsa at fourteen, or whenever they feel ready. Believers avoid alcohol and tobacco. They encourage hospitality to strangers, so Sikh temples have kitchens for hungry visitors and rooms where travelers can sleep. In the temples, believers sing hymns to God and read from their scripture, the Sri Guru Granth Sahib, which is the spiritual poetry of all God's teachers.

The First Church of Christ, Unitarian, in Lancaster, Massachusetts; each element represents nature and strong ties to the natural world; the flaming chalice symbolizes the warmth of community as the fire of creative truth drawn from an eternal cup; the two circles represent the joining of Unitarianism and Universalism.

Unitarian

Christians who did not believe in God as three—Father, Son and Holy Ghost—cropped up all over Europe among Protestants in the sixteenth century. Some were even burned at the stake for heresy. So when an American preacher, William Ellery Channing, gave his sermon one wintry day in 1819, his hands were shaking. For the last few years, people in New England had been arguing about whether Jesus was God and how much humans had to rely on God. Channing told the congregation that Jesus was a prophetic teacher with a spark of divinity in him but was not God. All people have the same spark, he said. He urged his listeners to look for God inside themselves. Channing was the first to use the word "Unitarian," meaning "one," as an alternative to "Trinitarian, or "three." Though many people rejected Channing's ideas at first, eventually many of America's oldest churches converted to Unitarianism.

Unitarians, who merged with the Universalists in 1961, emphasize the importance of the mind and education. They believe people need to find their own paths to God. They also believe in the goodness of the Earth and all its inhabitants. All people are important and should be treated fairly and kindly. The Bible is only one source of truth among many, they say. Most Unitarians have no official religious ceremonies or prescribed doctrines but direct their energies toward establishing peace and justice in the world.

Rural huts in Africa; weaving; carvings used in ancestor worship.

Yoruba

Before the Earth was created, the world was nothing but a sea of lava, said the Yoruba people, living along the Niger River in Africa. So the supreme being, Olodumare, sent orisa to create dry land. The orisa descended to Earth on an iron chain. They shaped the rivers, hills, trees, flowers, and birds. After they finished, the spirits entered their creations, making all things alive. Then God breathed the life force into human beings. But the male deities forgot to include Osun, goddess of the water. So Olodumare ordered them to return and make peace with Osun, who made use of her powers to ensure that the work of creation and populating the world was complete. To honor these gods, Yoruba people offered a sacrifice—perhaps fruit, flowers, candles, or favorite foods. For life's biggest problems, they sacrificed animals. Starting in the seventeenth century, many Yoruba were brought to the Americas as slaves, where they adopted the Catholicism of their owners. Yet, they managed to hold onto their Yoruba spiritual traditions, which influenced other groups that evolved into Macumba, Condomble, Ifa and vodou.

In modern times, the Yoruba still embrace a supreme god, also called Olorun, and hundreds of orisa. They believe in reincarnation within a family, and that good behavior maintains a balance among the spirits. Family members who have died return often to check in with the living, particularly during annual Egungun festivals. While the Yoruba people make up a sizable majority of West Africa, followers now can be found in the U.S., Canada and the Caribbean as well. Though they often practice a faith blended with Christianity or Islam, underneath the Yoruba honor their orisa with processions, pilgrimages, and prayer.

Light symbolizes righteousness; wings represent the divinity that exists in every person; fire symbolizes God and truth.

Zoroastrian

A long time before Muhammad, Jesus, or even Buddha, the prophet Zoroaster lived in Persia (now Iran). He had many visions in which he learned that the world is ruled by one supreme god, Ahura Mazda, who is in an eternal battle with an evil power called Angra Mainyu. Ahura Mazda created the world and human beings to help him in the struggle. People must choose whom to follow. Goodness will triumph, Zoroaster taught, when people follow the threefold path of good thoughts, good works, and good deeds. After death, each soul will cross a bridge that widens to help righteous people in their journey toward heaven but becomes razor-thin for the wicked, causing them to drop into a dark pit.

Fire represents God and truth, Zoroastrians (including some groups in India who are called Parsis or Irini) believe, and so a fire burns in their temples at all times. They pray five times each day, facing the light. At age seven, boys and girls receive a white undershirt to wear the rest of their lives as a sign of faith. They also get a sacred cord which is wrapped around their waist three times, reminding them of their connection to God. At marriage, a priest uses a similar string to encircle the couple, symbolizing their unity. With these acts, Zoroastrians show their love of God and their willingness to fight against evil.

Thatched house called Indus; club and spear are battle gear; Zulu ceremonies include dancing and singing with power and exuberance. Border: shield; triangle represents the father, mother and child; triangle pointing down represents an unmarried woman; pointing up it represents an unmarried man.

Zulu

Living on the southern tip of Africa, the Zulu ("sky" and "heaven") people believed that the all-powerful, supreme and supernatural God, known as Unkulunkulu ("the Great One"), emerged from a huge wetland of reeds to shape the world. This god then filled the land and the water with humans, animals, plants and all living things. But Unkulunkulu was a distant god, who didn't interfere in the lives of people. Meanwhile, they learned of the female goddess, Mbaba Mwana Waresa, who did control human and harvest fertility. She is also known as Nomkhubulwane, who could transform herself into various animals. Ancestor spirits—who could be benevolent and malevolent—would visit the living through dreams or in the form of a snake.

In their South African kingdom today, the Zulu teach that people are complex creatures, with bodies, souls, emotions, and brains, but also a shadow side that produces negative emotions. Zulus perform "thanksgiving" offerings for a happy outcome, like a good harvest or the birth of a baby. There is another ritual for "scolding" the spirits for bad luck, an unexpected death or when things go wrong. Spirits visit during key moments of a person's mortal journey—birth, puberty, marriage and death. Growing old is considered a gift from the gods, so the elderly are held in high esteem. Death is not the end, the Zulu believe, but a transition. In their societies, they cultivate and reinforce their values by singing and story-telling, reading and remembering, beading and believing, as they navigate heaven and earth.

The Golden Rule
as taught in many traditions

Baha'i

"Ascribe not to any soul
that which thou wouldst
not have ascribed to
thee, and say not that
which thou doest not."
—Bahá'u'lláh
Hidden Words, Arabic 29

Buddhism

"Just as you did for
yourself, likewise do
the same for others too."
—Buddha
Udanāvarga 23:8

Christianity

"Do unto others as
you would have them
do unto you."
—Jesus
The Bible, Luke 6:31

Confucianism

"Do not do to others
what you do not want
done to yourself."
—Confucius
The Analects 15:23

Hinduism

"Do not to others what
ye do not wish done to
yourself. This is the whole
Dharma; heed it well."
—Sage Vyasa
The Mahābhārata 5:1517

Islam

"No one of you is a
believer until you desire
for another that which
you desire for yourself."
—Muhammad
An-Nawawi, Hadīth 13

Judaism

"What is hateful to
you, do not do to your
neighbor. That is the
entire Torah; the rest
is commentary."
—Rabbi Hillel
Babylonian Talmud, Shabbat 31a

Native American

"Respect for all life
is the foundation."
—Deganawidah
The Great Law of Peace

Sikhism

"Be not estranged from
another, for in every
heart pervades the Lord."
—Guru Arjan Dev
Sri Guru Granth Sahib

Zoroastrianism

"Human nature is good
only when it does not do
unto another whatever is
not good for its own self."
—Manuskihar
Dādistān-ī-Dīnīk 94:5

Our thanks to Professor Dorothy Marcic of Vanderbilt University for bringing these quotations to our attention. They are in her book, *Managing with the Wisdom of Love: Uncovering Virtue in People and Organizations*, published by Jossey-Bass.

Peggy Fletcher Stack, award-winning religion writer for The Salt Lake Tribune, has reported from six continents, was on the team that won a Pulitzer for the paper, and was a founding member of the International Association of Religion Journalists. She has interviewed Buddhist teachers and Baha'i believers, Catholic cardinals and Protestant pastors, Muslim imams and Jewish rabbis—as well as the folk in every faith. Covering religion has been her passion.

Artist **Kathleen Bateman Peterson** was born in the Rocky Mountains and has lived in Hawaii and Malaysia and painted in Central America, Nepal, and Thailand. She has illustrated over 25 books on a variety of topics, including "Girls Who Choose God: Stories of Courageous Women From the Bible." Her paintings can be found in galleries in Utah and Hawaii, or at kathleenpetersonart.com. She lives and paints on a farm in Spring City, Utah.

Made in the USA
Monee, IL
18 February 2023

82393c97-d322-40d4-b0c9-793809589d95R01